What Am I Bound To?

Sarle' Jeffries

BookLeaf Publishing

India | USA | UK

What Am I Bound To? © 2024 Sarle' Jeffries

All rights reserved.

Sarle' Jeffries asserts the moral right to be identified as the author of this work.

Presentation by *BookLeaf Publishing*

Web: www.bookleafpub.com

E-mail: info@bookleafpub.com

ISBN: 9789360940706

First edition 2024

*For every Soul who has ever felt the weight of
shame and the warmth of pleasure.*

*For those who bravely navigate the spaces
between vulnerability and strength.*

*For all those who align with me, naturally or
through effort.*

This book is dedicated to you.

ACKNOWLEDGEMENT

Appreciation for the contributions of every participant between New York, the DMV, and Atlanta.
Y'all invested your Time, Energy, Effort & Vessels to be a part of the "What Are You Bound To?" series. Your willingness to share yourselves with me, for trusting me with your truths, and for allowing me to weave them in the fabric of this collection is valued.

And to the readers who are holding this book in their hands, thank you.
May these words remind you of our interconnectedness and inspire you to explore what you are bound to and all that you're bound to that liberates you.

With Gratitude,

Sarle'

PREFACE

Originally conceived as an Art x Social Justice project, "What Are You Bound To?" began as a pilgrimage to return to my why's through the exploration of shame and pleasure. These verbal and visual dialogues highlighted the complexities of shame and aimed to unravel the narratives that shape our lives and bind us to our pasts.
At its core, is a journey that began with the desire to connect.
Through creating and observing how spaces are used between the intersection of creativity and expressionism, "What Am I Bound To?" emerges from a vision to explore this conversation through poetry and storytelling.

What Am I Bound To?

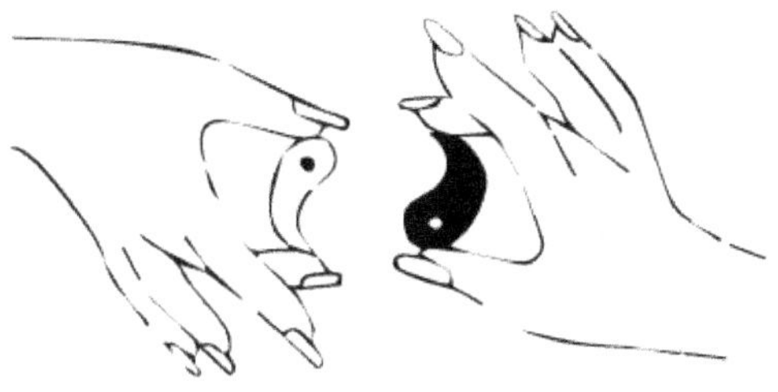

I am constantly engaged in the work of the
thread &
The (In)Visible Nature of Interconnectedness…

I'm beckoned to witness
the tapestry that is woven between our roots,
weaved with our emotional fabric,
and reinforced with our physical, social,
and Energetic patterns.

And in it recognize,
I am an Influence of it.
To it.

.The Fixed Formula.

How I Breathe x
How I Think   x
How I Move
=

Product of (my) Being

You'll Always Be Attached Through Me: A Letter to my Mother

You held me as I entered this world,
And I held you as you left it.
I'm Grateful for the Trust.

While simultaneously still being very much IN
the experience
of learning how to live without you,
I believe I'll forever be in the seasons
of filling what's been emptied in your absence.

Meeting you in my memories,
Honoring you in Rituals—
I hold space for the time we shared.
Thank you.
I am the Evidence of your Motherhood,
and as a result, the Influence of your Love.

Adorning the Flesh

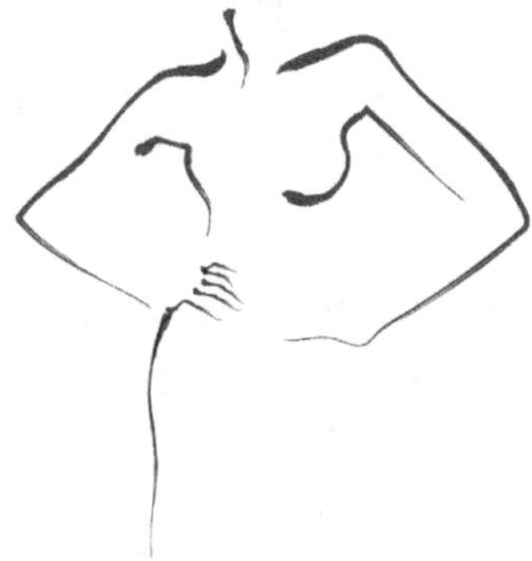

I'm attached to the Journey my Flesh has taken
on—
My Ink Stains are Visual Poetry.
They spoke for me and to me before I was
ready—
Much like symbols do.
Connecting meaning with feeling
and intention with representation—
They speak to the development pattern of my
system of beliefs.

Recently someone asked me which tattoo is my
favorite.
My natural response was to hold myself tightly
and say,
"Shhhh, they'll hear you."

After we chuckled a good chuckle and they
entertained my need for them to reframe the
question;
they asked,
"Which three tattoos are you the most attached
to in this current moment?"

The three I selected:
First, my Nyansapo.
The wisdom knot.
Centered to Cultivate my Qi.
Between the Upper and Lower Dantian
Marked on me after my Mother's death.
Second, a Portal on the dorsal side of my right
hand.
This Circle concentrates my Currency—
And is a consistent reminder to be Focused on
what I want to Birth.
Third, on the inside of my right bicep there are
two vessels involved in ritual.
Those two Spirits entwined Intimately.
Symbolizing my Active Outward Energy.

The Skin I'm in/Flesh Adorned

Cutting
Ties

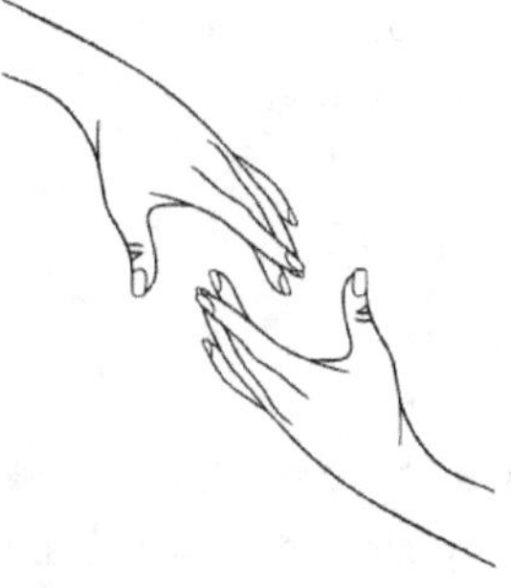

Sometimes letting go
Starts with being let go of.

I'm Connected to My Perspective:
Part I

A conversation with a tree:
She called me over much like an endearing Sage
would,
In a sweetness that was difficult to ignore.
I observed Her roots rising and falling through
multiple levels of the ground,
like the veins in the hands of an elder's skin.
I sat at the ground that was crumbling beneath
Her
and was able to see how far her roots stretched.
They reached into other trees and around
rocks—
I continued to follow them
until I could no longer fathom how much Deeper
she traveled.

She listened to me for some time, and I listened
to Her.
We created and shared silence.

Before we parted, with compassion she
imparted…
"Do not be fooled by the ground you stand on.
Sometimes it must break apart for you to truly
witness the richness of your essence."
I thanked her then and thank her now.
I never forgot this exchange and we still talk
when I visit.

When I have the desire to be embraced, I return
to Nature.

Insecurities I'm Attached to—

I have a missing side tooth.

But I still smile wide!
Using all my teeth:
To grin in the face of adversity,
Chuckle with Joy and
Laugh alongside my courage.

Mwah Ha Ha

*I Attach Through Multiple Portals *

Think of all the windows you've ever sat at.

Which one was your favorite?

Tell me why…

Now tell me—
Out of all the windows you thought of,
Were they open or closed?

There are moments within my current reality
where

I am transferred back to a particular window I
couldn't see far out of.
All the best memories gathered there were with
my eyes shut and my mind open.
I collected many dreams and traveled to many
alter planes from there.
My bed was perched right next to the window,
whose gap enhanced my rest.
I can still taste the air, sensing the energy of
movement stirring my body's response.
I can feel the transition between night and day, I
can smell the humidity.
It's typhoon season in Japan.
I'm transported back to The Black Album,
Speakerboxx/TheLoveBelow,
The Diary of Alicia Keys,
Dangerously in Love,
Get Rich or Die Trying,
Worldwide Underground
and the expected daily noise of reveille.

I'm back at this opening of my memory.
Viewing myself from the other side of this
experience.
Looking through the window at myself, of my
past,
through the portal of my senses…
Watching myself sleep.

Enjoying my dreams, through the only set of
closed windows I admire.

! I'm Bound to Nature...

The Nature of my Selves
The Nature of my Mind
The Nature of Reality
and
The Nature of Death

Lessons I Give Myself Grace For

Sometimes...

Detachment is a long game.

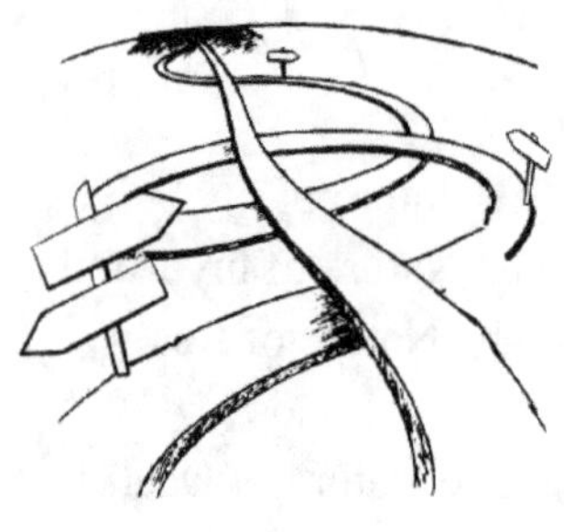

***

The
Elements
of
Connection

***

I'm Bound to the Rhythms of the Universe—
While Being a Co-creator of my own.

I am Bound to the Bidirectional Experience of
my Senses.

The relationship I have with time is vital to my
perspectives.
The relationship I have with space is vital to my
body.

Sometimes fire resonates through me.
Sometimes water resonates through me.
Sometimes the earth resonates through me.
I'm always Air.

Guided through the Energies.

Fire Gives,
Water Receives,
Earth Grounds,
Air Flows—
following the path it creates.
Spirit Connects All.

****

****

And in the process,
I've disconnected myself from the belief
that I have to FILL space.
It is just as powerful to empty.

I'm Connected to My Perspective: Part II

It's only a problem if you don't have a solution.

I have a wealth of resources because I'm Resourceful.

Everything Exists in Degrees of Vibration.

A Mantra

I Am Bound to the Vision of my Desires.

Bound to my Requests:

Keep your worries over there…
Do not mask your doubt as concern for me.

Drown yourself in the tension of your fears.

I'll be over here—
learning how to float above the bullshit,
swim through the challenges,
and navigate these lessons.

NOTE TO SELF

Ego Death = Ego Life

.Connection Points.

There are Portals through my Touch
There are Portals through my Soles

They Guide me to Join Spontaneously,
Move Alternatively,
Love Naturally and
Unite with Purpose in Mind.

It's where Qi Enters
Flowing through the channels within me
Influencing when I am the wave and when I'm
riding the wave.

I'm Connected to My Perspective:
Part III

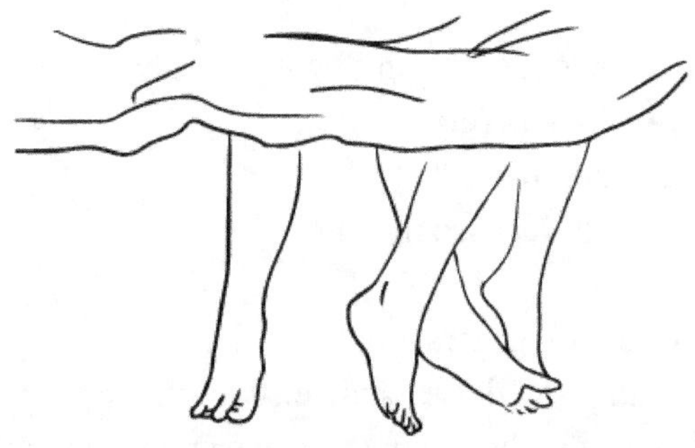

I am Bound to my Body.

I Learn through my Erotic Curiosity.

I am an Electromagnetic being...

We all exist as a Lightwave,
set with a code of frequencies reassimilated by
recognizable versions of ourselves,
Outlined by the courage to pursue our desires.

Bound to Structure:
A Haiku

Everything I touch
Is Guided by Trust within—
That expands outwards.

The Impact of a Date

I've never been big on Birthday celebrations.
When I got to a certain age,
I began taking my mother out on OUR birthing
day
and that became our ritual.
It was a sensation.
My giving thanks for safe passage while
sharing time to acknowledge our Journey
together over an Apple Martini.

But before that—
The first birthday party I remember having, I
was 12.
And I mostly remember the pictures of it.
Me smiling wide, sitting on my mother's lap
grinning.
Then there was my 16th, my high school
boyfriend planned a surprise party for me at my
folks' house—
but I don't remember the party.
I remember that in my haste before the surprise,
I caused a slight fender bender between my car
and his dads.
On my 17th, I went to the recruiter's station and
enlisted in the Marine Corps.

With my dad next to me, excitedly beaming in
pride,
I met Staff Sergeant Goodwater then had lunch
at Applebee's.
On my 18th, I was stationed in Japan.
I spent the day doing laundry and talking to my
Mom on the phone.
I can still smell the detergent's smell rising in
the heat from the dryers.

Our 36th celebration.
I spent it in the hospital with you and gave you
lap dances.
Now enter 37.
It's the first occurrence of me remembering as
many details
about a single time-frame.

I remember asking her in the beginning of
February if She would make it with me to my
birthday.
I can still see her face as she slightly dropped
her head and softly shook her head from left to
right.
I held her hand and said, "Ok Mommy, that's
alright. I've had 36 with you."
And I hugged her.
Because WE needed it.

My mom was nonverbal the last two days of her
life.
I filled the space talking to Her.
I'm glad I did.
I don't remember many dates, but I'll always
remember.

My Mom passed 2.8
Her funeral was 2.15
My birth date is 2.18
My mother's birth date is 3.8
And my eldest daughter's birth date is 3.18

Δ

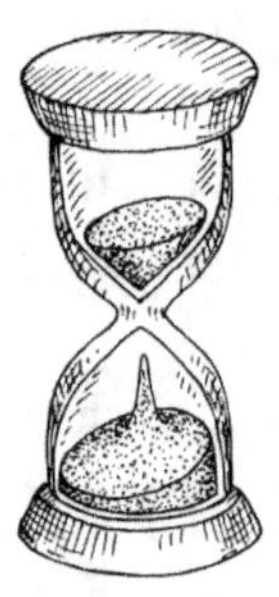

More Shit I'm Bound To

I'm Bound to my culture, that is the rhythm
behind my breath, how I move, and sing.

I'm Bound to the traditions that eased me into
sight and taught me how to listen.

I'm Bound to the languages I've never learned
but speak in my dreams.

I'm Bound to the moments in life that changed
my perspective.

I'm Bound to the thread of life that will return
me to my death.

I'm Bound to letting go of beliefs that do not
serve me.

I'm Bound to the idea that safety is an illusion.

I'm Bound to the fluidity of detachment.

I'm Bound to emptying so I can fill.

I'm Bound to my vision.

I'm Bound to self.

I'm Bound.

Bound.

Free.

*** I'm Secure in My Joy

***

Laughter Restores.

Laughter Alleviates.

Laughter has a rhythm that interrupts the sound waves around you.

The Body is enlightened through Laughter.

How do you listen?

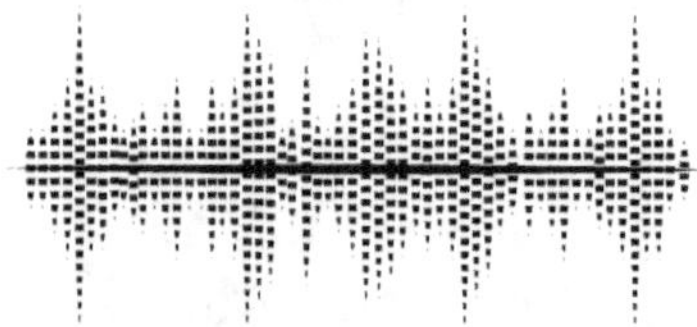

There are layers to sound.
When you peel them back,
What does it reveal?
The absence of silence—
or the ingredients for its creation?
Quiet is when you catch the gap in the rhythm,
a part of the cycle that reminds you of its power.
Oscillating and vibrating your sensory system
only to dissect and accumulate through
awareness…
that is the catalyst to HOW we hear.
We can be exposed to the same wavelengths
and we will interpret them differently
through the cycles and rhythms
of how it resonates with our patterns.
And when there's nothing left to hear,
We are left with the vibrations of our heart
beating.

Rules of a Shadow Guide

How I nurture
Is by instilling courage for you to see
yourselves.

The essential flow is in guiding others to
discovering their goodness—
So, they may create the foundation of their
integrity.

Along the journey of aligning to the truth of who
you are and what you can do,
I'm there.

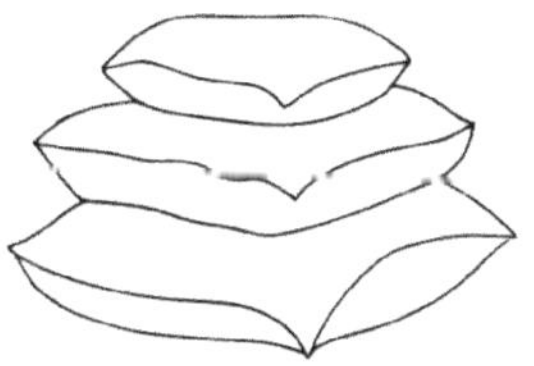

"Thas Why Yah Got Bones"

I observed myself through the wildness of my
tears.
Puddled on the ground unable to move,
unsure of how I could make the next attempt to
move a limb.
I laughed.
A deep laugh.
I was paralyzed in my emotions.

I kept telling myself, the least I could do was
breathe with intention.
To not lose control of my body's ability to
breathe.
I laid there,
crying,
laughing some more,
dancing between the intensities of the emotions
and then—

Managed to form silence...

I gathered my voice... I asked for help. I said,
"I can't move... I need help. I can't even stand
right now."

And that's when clear as day,

I heard a visitor say with a thick southern accent,

"Thas why yah got Bones."

I closed my eyes and remembered the stories I
collected from my tribe
about all the ancestors who live in your joints.
Upholding you through your journey,
Your bones are about your history,
Your muscles are about your present,
and your breath is about your future...

I got lost in these thoughts and felt the collective
energy urging me to get up when I was ready
and reminding me,

"Thas why yah got bones."

****
*****

Give thanks for all that holds me up when I am
not able.

Will You Listen?

I speak in touch,
In gaze,
In rhythm.

***A Road To Remedy ***

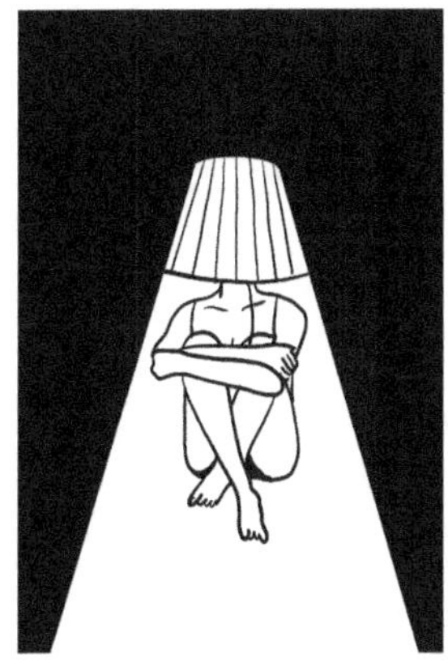

Reflect

Release

Revisit

Reapply

Root

Rest

Repeat